DATE: MAY 26, 2003

FROM: KAREN

TO: KATHY

MESSAGE: HAVE A HAPPY
BIRTHDAY!

❦ MESSAGES OF FRIENDSHIP ❦

I Wish You All the Best

Text by Helmut Walch

Photography by Andrew Cowin

ABBEVILLE PRESS PUBLISHERS

NEW YORK   LONDON   PARIS

All the treasures in the world

I wish for you, as many as you wish. But the greatest

treasure of humankind lies not in the things we possess;

it lies in simply being. And in this way I wish you an

embarrassment of riches.

I wish you courage. Courage to traverse unfamiliar paths when you must, courage to try new things, courage to strive for excellence. Don't let fear of the unknown command your decisions; let it be courage.

You should never lose hope.

Hope is the fire that warms us before we set out on a journey, it's the rain that nourishes the thirsty ground so that new flowers may blossom in unexpected places.

❦

It's not always easy to share.

May you always find the ability to communicate with

spirit, heart, and feeling so that others may understand

and accept.

I hope you will never want for friends, for kindred spirits with whom you can exchange thoughts, and for friendly opposition, so that you may widen your horizons.

I hope a person who feels love and affection toward you will enter your life. A person you can depend on and lean on in times of need, a person who brings you peace and renewed strength.

❧

The art of forgiveness is rare.

It requires dignity and is a sign of spiritual nobility.

My wish for you is to cultivate this noble ability, for

your own well-being as well as your friends'.

Taking the plunge is half the battle, as the saying goes. Still, we don't always have the momentum we need to get going. May you always find the drive you need in the crucial moment.

There are times when mak-ing a decision seems all too overwhelming, situations when experience is needed. May you always find the maturity to rise to the occasion.

My wish for you is that you will always be willing to help others—not merely out of a sense of duty, but because it brings you sincere pleasure and enriches your life.

Health may not be everything, but without your health everything is nothing. I needn't say more; you already know my wish for you. Still, it doesn't hurt for me to give you a little reminder to take care of yourself.

I wish that you may begin each day with a smile, because then the game is already halfway won. Stake your claim to happiness and use its power of persuasion.

Remember to allow yourself some leisure time. When the moment is right, it should be possible for you to cast aside your worries and enjoy the benefits of time spent your own way.

To tilt at windmills and swim against the tide are exhausting and fruitless pursuits. I wish for you the insight to know how to remain flexible.

It doesn't matter if you believe

in guardian angels or other creatures who protect you—

when you can't go on, when you've hit bottom, help will

come from above.

❦

When you succeed in learning to love the good things in life, your senses are enriched all the more. May color, shapes, sounds, scents, and tastes always bring you joy.

With each passing year, with each passing day, we grow older. Age is not merely a measuring of time. My wish for you is to remain young at heart and in mind.

❦

If life leads you to a fork in the road, you'll need courage to make a decision. Harder still will be choosing the right direction. I hope you'll always have a good sense of your bearings so the decision will be easy for you.

❦

Life's never-ending ups and downs can be enthralling, but also tiring. And so I wish you a sense of balance so that you—and your family and friends—may stay on an even keel.

❦

One of the most important things in life is to set a goal and pursue it with all you've got. May you always cross the finish line.

❦